Thirty Ways to Enter Paradise

From the Qur'an and the Sunnah

Hiba.

Al-Firdous Ltd.

2001: First Edition

Typeset by Abu Yusuf.

ISBN 1 874263 66 3

Available from: and from

Al-Firdous Ltd.,   Ta-Ha Publishers Ltd.,
10 Fonthill Road   1 Wynne Road
London, N4 3HX   London SW9 0BB

Email: books@al-firdous.co.uk
Web-Site: www.al-firdous.co.uk

All praise is due to Allah. We praise Him, seek His Aid and ask for His Forgiveness. We seek Allah's Refuge from the evils of ourselves and from the evil of our actions. Whomsoever Allah guides none can lead astray, and whomsoever Allah leads astray none can guide. I testify that none has the right to be worshipped but Allah Alone, having no partners, and I testify that Muhammad is His Slave and Messenger.

This is a booklet entitled "Thirty Ways to Enter Paradise", in which I have accumulated a number of Verses and Sound Ahadith, which deal with the deeds that enable a believer to enter paradise, by Allah's Will. However, this does not mean that any person who fulfils these deeds can secure himself a place in Paradise, no matter what faith he or she believes in. Paradise is but rewarded to the true believers. For example, if an unbeliever or a polytheist fulfils some or all of these deeds, it will be of no avail to him and will not make him or her enter paradise, because Allah ﷻ says, **⟨and indeed it has been revealed to you (O Muhammad ﷺ), as it was to those before you: "If you join others in worship with Allah, surely all your deeds will be in vain, and you will certainly be among the losers⟩** (*Az-Zumar*: **65**). Also, Allah ﷻ says of the disbelievers, **⟨and We shall turn to whatever deeds they (disbelievers, polytheists) did, and We shall make such deeds as scattered floating particles of dust⟩** (*Al-Furqaan*: 23).

Therefore, Islam is the first condition for the acceptance of any deed.

The second condition is sincerity; for any deed to be accepted by Allah ﷻ, it should be done sincerely and for the Cause of Allah ﷻ. A believer should not join any creature with Allah in his/her intention to do any deed. The Prophet ﷺ said: "Allah ﷻ does not accept a deed except for that which is done entirely for His Cause and through which one seeks Allah's Pleasure." [1]

---

[1] Reported by an-Nasa'i, "*Sahih al-Ja'mi*'" 1856.

The third condition for a deed to be accepted is by following the Prophet ﷺ; therefore, I have only relied on the Sound Ahadith of the Prophet ﷺ.

I ask Allah ﷻ to make this humble work for His Sake, and to reward me, as well as my family and all Muslims, on the Day when neither wealth nor sons will avail any man, except for him who brings to Allah a clean heart. If I do right, it is only by the Help of Allah, but if I err, it is from Satan and myself.

I testify that there is no god but Allah, Glory be to Him, and that Muhammad ﷺ is His Messenger. Peace and Blessings be upon our Prophet ﷺ, his family and all his Companions.

Thirty Ways To Enter Paradise From The Qur'an and The Sunnah

The First and Second Ways
Faith and Good Deeds

Allah ﷻ makes mention of Faith (*Eemaan*) in the Noble Qur'an as the main reason that leads to Paradise, by Allah's Leave. However, *Eemaan* is always accompanied by good deeds; therefore, whenever *Eemaan* is mentioned in the Qur'an, it is associated with good deeds, as the main action that leads to Paradise. There are many ways to do good deeds and to earn rewards for them, which only Allah ﷻ knows of. Allah ﷻ says:

وَٱلَّذِينَ ءَامَنُوا۟ وَعَمِلُوا۟ ٱلصَّٰلِحَٰتِ أُو۟لَٰٓئِكَ أَصْحَٰبُ ٱلْجَنَّةِ هُمْ فِيهَا خَٰلِدُونَ ﴿٨٢﴾

❨Those who believe and do righteous deeds, they are dwellers of Paradise, they will dwell therein forever❩ (Al-Baqarah: 82).

There are many Verses and Ahadith, which talk about *Eemaan* and good deeds as being the reason for entering Paradise, such as: Surat al-Baqarah: verses 25 and 82; Surat Luqmaan: verse 8; Surat al-Kahf: verse 107; Surat al-Hajj: verses 14, 23 and 56; Surat al-Fat'h: verse 5; Surat al-Hadid: verses 12 and 21; Surat at-Taghabun: verse 9; Surat at-Talaaq: verse 11; Surat al-Buruj: verse 11; Surat al-Bayyinah: verse 7; Surat al-Mu'minun: verses 1 and 11 and Surat al-Ankabut: verse 57.

The Third Way
Piety (Taqwa')

Taqwa' is to fear Allah, abide by His Book (the Qur'an), be content with little and be prepared for death. *Taqwa'* is also defined as: the obedience of Allah ﷻ through His Light (the Qur'an and Sunnah of His Prophet ﷺ), seeking His Reward, abandoning unlawful deeds and fearing His Punishment.

For more information about the meaning of *Taqwa'*, see Ibn Al-Qayyim's "*Ighathatu al-Luhfaan*" and "*Madarij as-Salikin*".

Allah ﷻ says:

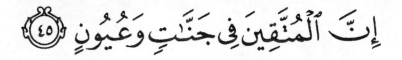

❨truly, the pious will be amidst Gardens and water-springs❩ (Al-Hijr: 45)

and He ﷻ also says:

وَسَارِعُوٓاْ إِلَىٰ مَغْفِرَةٍ مِّن رَّبِّكُمْ وَجَنَّةٍ عَرْضُهَا ٱلسَّمَٰوَٰتُ وَٱلْأَرْضُ أُعِدَّتْ لِلْمُتَّقِينَ ۝

{and be quick for forgiveness from your Lord, and for Paradise as wide as are the heavens and the earth, prepared for the pious} (Aal-Imran: 133).

The Prophet ﷺ said: "Do you know the thing which most commonly brings people into Paradise? It is fear of Allah (*Taqwa'*) and good character. Do you know what most commonly brings people into Hell? It is the two hollow things: the mouth and the private parts." This Hadith is narrated by at-Tirmidhi, Ibn Majah and Imam Ahmed.

The Fourth Way

Obedience to Allah ﷻ and His Messenger ﷺ

Allah ﷻ says:

لَّيۡسَ عَلَى ٱلۡأَعۡمَىٰ حَرَجٞ وَلَا عَلَى ٱلۡأَعۡرَجِ حَرَجٞ وَلَا عَلَى ٱلۡمَرِيضِ حَرَجٞ وَمَن يُطِعِ ٱللَّهَ وَرَسُولَهُۥ يُدۡخِلۡهُ جَنَّٰتٖ تَجۡرِي مِن تَحۡتِهَا ٱلۡأَنۡهَٰرُ وَمَن يَتَوَلَّ يُعَذِّبۡهُ عَذَابًا أَلِيمٗا ﴿١٧﴾

❰ No blame or sin is upon the blind, nor is there blame or sin upon the lame, nor is there blame or sin upon the sick. And whosoever obeys Allah and His Messenger, He will admit him to Gardens beneath which rivers flow; and

12

whosoever turns back, He will punish him with a painful torment (Al-Fat'h: 17).

It is reported in Sahih al-Bukhari, on the authority of Abu Hurairah ﷺ, that the Prophet ﷺ said: "All my followers will enter Paradise except those who refuse." They said, "O Allah's Apostle! Who will refuse?" He ﷺ said, "Whoever obeys me will enter Paradise, and whoever disobeys me is the one who refuses (to enter it)." (*Fast'h al-Bari*: 13/249).

The Fifth Way
Jihad in Allah's Cause

Jihad in Allah's Cause is fulfilled by giving our wealth and lives in the Cause of Allah ﷻ. Allah ﷻ says:

۞ إِنَّ ٱللَّهَ ٱشْتَرَىٰ مِنَ ٱلْمُؤْمِنِينَ أَنفُسَهُمْ وَأَمْوَٰلَهُم بِأَنَّ لَهُمُ ٱلْجَنَّةَ يُقَٰتِلُونَ فِى سَبِيلِ ٱللَّهِ فَيَقْتُلُونَ وَيُقْتَلُونَ وَعْدًا عَلَيْهِ حَقًّا فِى ٱلتَّوْرَىٰةِ وَٱلْإِنجِيلِ وَٱلْقُرْءَانِ وَمَنْ أَوْفَىٰ بِعَهْدِهِۦ مِنَ ٱللَّهِ فَٱسْتَبْشِرُوا۟ بِبَيْعِكُمُ ٱلَّذِى بَايَعْتُم بِهِۦ وَذَٰلِكَ هُوَ ٱلْفَوْزُ ٱلْعَظِيمُ ۝

❨Verily, Allah has purchased from the believers their lives and their properties, for the price that theirs shall be Paradise. They fight in Allah's Cause, so they kill and are killed. It is a

14

promise, in truth, which is binding on Him in the Torah, the Gospel and the Qur'an . And who is truer to his covenant than Allah? Then rejoice in the bargain which you have concluded. That is the supreme success ❭ (At-Tawbah: 111).

Allah ﷻ also says:

$$يَـٰٓأَيُّهَا ٱلَّذِينَ ءَامَنُوا۟ هَلۡ أَدُلُّكُمۡ عَلَىٰ تِجَـٰرَةٍ تُنجِيكُم مِّنۡ عَذَابٍ أَلِيمٍ ۝ تُؤۡمِنُونَ بِٱللَّهِ وَرَسُولِهِۦ وَتُجَـٰهِدُونَ فِى سَبِيلِ ٱللَّهِ بِأَمۡوَٰلِكُمۡ وَأَنفُسِكُمۡ ذَٰلِكُمۡ خَيۡرٌ لَّكُمۡ إِن كُنتُمۡ تَعۡلَمُونَ ۝ يَغۡفِرۡ لَكُمۡ ذُنُوبَكُمۡ وَيُدۡخِلۡكُمۡ جَنَّـٰتٍ تَجۡرِى مِن تَحۡتِهَا ٱلۡأَنۡهَـٰرُ وَمَسَـٰكِنَ طَيِّبَةً فِى جَنَّـٰتِ عَدۡنٍ ذَٰلِكَ ٱلۡفَوۡزُ ٱلۡعَظِيمُ ۝$$

❴O you who believe! Shall I show you a commerce that will save you from a painful doom? You should believe in Allah and His Messenger, and should strive for the cause of Allah with your wealth and your lives. That is better for you, if you did but know. He will forgive you your sins and bring you into

15

Gardens underneath which rivers flow, and pleasant dwellings in Gardens of Eden. That is the supreme triumph〉 (As-Saff: 10-12).

The Sixth Way

Sincere Repentance (At-Tawbah)

Sincere repentance washes away previous sins, as the Prophet ﷺ said: "A person who sincerely seeks repentance from a sin that he/she has committed is like one who has committed no sin." This Hadith is reported by Ibn Majah and others, "*Sahih al-Ja'mi*" 3008.

Allah ﷻ says:

$$إِلَّا مَن تَابَ وَءَامَنَ وَعَمِلَ صَلِحًا فَأُوْلَٰٓئِكَ يَدْخُلُونَ ٱلْجَنَّةَ وَلَا يُظْلَمُونَ شَيْئًا ٦٠$$

❴except those who repent and believe, and do righteousness. Such will enter Paradise and they will not be wronged in aught❵ (Maryam: 60).

The Seventh Way

Standing firm and Straight upon Allah's Religion

Allah ﷻ says:

إِنَّ ٱلَّذِينَ قَالُوا۟ رَبُّنَا
ٱللَّهُ ثُمَّ ٱسْتَقَـٰمُوا۟ فَلَا خَوْفٌ عَلَيْهِمْ وَلَا هُمْ يَحْزَنُونَ ۝
أُو۟لَـٰٓئِكَ أَصْحَـٰبُ ٱلْجَنَّةِ خَـٰلِدِينَ فِيهَا جَزَآءًۢ بِمَا كَانُوا۟ يَعْمَلُونَ ۝

❨verily, those who say: "Our Lord is Allah," and therefore *Istaqaamu* (stood firm and straight on the Islamic Faith), on them shall be no fear, nor shall they grieve. Such shall be the dwellers of Paradise, abiding therein forever, a reward for what they used to do❩ (Al-Ahqaaf: 13-14).

Sufyan Ibn Abdullah ath-Thaqafi said: "I asked the Messenger of Allah ﷺ, 'tell me about something in Islam which might dispense with the necessity of my asking anybody after you.' He ﷺ said: "Say, 'I affirm my faith in Allah,' and then remain steadfast to it." This Hadith is narrated by Imam Muslim.

The Eighth Way

Seeking Knowledge for Allah's Sake

On the authority of Abu Hurairah ﷺ, the Prophet ﷺ said: "He who treads the path in search of knowledge, Allah will make that path easy, leading to Paradise, for him and those persons who assemble in one of the houses of Allah (mosques) to recite the Book of Allah and learn and teach the Qur'an (among themselves). There will descend upon them tranquility, mercy will cover them, the angels will surround them and Allah will mention them in the presence of those near Him. He who is slow-paced in doing good deeds, his (good) lineage will not help him to go ahead." Imam Muslim reported this Hadith.

The Ninth Way

Building of Mosques

It is confirmed in Sahih al-Bukhari, on the authority of Uthman Ibn Affan ﷺ, I heard the Prophet ﷺ say: "Whoever builds a mosque for Allah's Sake, Allah will build for him/her a similar place in Paradise."

The Tenth Way
Good Character

On the authority of Abu Umamah, the Prophet ﷺ said: "I guarantee a house in the surroundings of Paradise for a man who avoids quarrelling, even if he were in the right; a house in the middle of Paradise for a man who avoids lying, even if he were joking; and a house in the upper part of Paradise for a man who made his character good." This Hadith was narrated by Abu Dawud and ad-Diya', "*Sahih al-Ja'mi*" 1464.

Also, the Prophet ﷺ said, "Do you know the thing which most commonly brings people into Paradise? It is fear of Allah (*Taqwa'*) and good character. Do you know what most commonly brings people into Hell? It is the two hollow things: the mouth and the private parts." This Hadith is narrated by at-Tirmidhi, Ibn Majah and Imam Ahmed.

Good character encompasses several things, which Aishah', may Allah be pleased with her, summarized, when asked about the character of the Prophet ﷺ; she said: "His character was the Qur'an." The Prophet ﷺ is our example and model, whom Allah ﷻ has praised in Surat al-Qalam:

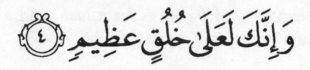

❴verily, you (Muhammad) are on an exalted standard of character❵ (verse 4).

Therefore, we should look at the Qur'an and the Sunnah of the Prophet ﷺ, and of his Companions to learn how to attain a good character. One of the best books that deals with the Prophet's ﷺ good character is Imam at-Tirmidhi's book "*Mukhtasar ash-Shama'il al-Muhammadiyyah*".

The Eleventh Way

Avoid Argument

The Prophet ﷺ said: "I guarantee a house in the surroundings of Paradise for a man who avoids quarrelling, even if he were in the right."

The Twelfth Way
Avoid Lying

The Prophet ﷺ said: "I guarantee a house in the surroundings of Paradise for a man who avoids quarrelling, even if he were in the right; a house in the middle of Paradise for a man who avoids lying, even if he were joking."

The Thirteenth Way

Ablution after Impurity and Praying two Rak'ahs after the Adhan

Imam at-Tirmidhi reported in his "*Sunan*", al-Hakim and Ibn Khuzaimah in his "*Sahih*", on the authority of Abdullah Ibn Buraidah ﷺ: "Buraydah ﷺ told how one morning Allah's Messenger ﷺ, called Bilal and said, 'What did you do to get to paradise before me? I have never entered paradise without hearing the rustling of your garments in front of me.' He replied, 'Messenger of Allah, I have never called the *Adhan* without praying two *Rak'ahs*, and no impurity has ever happened to me without my performing ablution on the spot and thinking that I owed Allah two *Rak'ahs*." Allah's Messenger

ﷺ said, "It is because of them." (*Sahih at-Targheeb Wat-Tarheeb* 194)

The Fourteen Way

Going to the Mosque for Congregational Salaat

On the authority of Abu Hurairah ﷺ, Imam Muslim and Imam al-Bukhari reported that the Prophet ﷺ said: "Allah will prepare for him who goes to the mosque (every) morning and in the afternoon (for the congregational prayer) an honourable place in Paradise, with good hospitality for (what he has done) going every morning and afternoon."

In his interpretation of this Hadith, Imam an-Nawawi, may Allah have Mercy upon him, said: "The Prophet's ﷺ saying: 'Allah ﷻ will prepare for him honourable places in Paradise', and a honourable place is what is prepared for the guest when he comes."

The Fifteen Way

Devoting Much Prostration to Allah

Imam Muslim narrated in his *"Sahih"*, on the authority of Rabi'ah Ibn Ka'b al-Aslami: "I was with Allah's Messenger ﷺ one night, and I brought him water and what he required. He said to me: 'Ask' (anything you like). I said: 'I ask for your company in Paradise.' He (the Prophet) ﷺ said: 'or for anything else besides it.' I said: 'That is all' (that I require). He ﷺ said: 'Then help me to achieve this for you; by devoting yourself often to prostration.'"

The Sixteen Way
Accepted Hajj

The Prophet ﷺ said: "Whoever performs *Hajj* to this House (*Ka'ba*) and does not approach his wife for sexual relations, nor commits sins (while performing *Hajj*), he will come out as sinless as a newly-born child. (Just delivered by his mother)." Al-Bukhari and others narrated this Hadith, see "*Faht al-Bari*", 3/382.

The Prophet ﷺ said: "An accepted *Hajj* has no reward, except Paradise." Imam Ahmed and Tabarani reported this Hadith, see: "*Sahih al-Ja'mi*'", 3170.

The Seventeenth Way

Reciting Aayat al-Kursi after each obligatory Salaat

Abu Uma'mah al-Bahili said: the Prophet ﷺ said: "Whoever recites *Aayat al-Kursi* after each obligatory *Salaat*, nothing stands on his way to Paradise, except death." An-Nisa'i, Ibn as-Suni and others narrated the above Hadith, see: "*As-Silsilah as-Sahihah*" 972.

Also, it is reported in Sahih al-Bukhari, on the authority of Shaddad Ibn Aws ﷺ, that the Prophet ﷺ said: "The most superior way of asking for forgiveness from Allah is: "'*Allahumma anta Rabbi la Ilaha illa anta, Anta Khalaqtani wa ana Abduka, wa ana 'ala ahdika wa wa'dika mastata'tu, A'udhu bika min Sharri ma sana'tu, abu'u Laka bini'matika 'alaiya, wa Abu'u Laka bidhanbi faghfirli innahu la yaghfiru adhdhunuba illa anta.'"*

The Prophet ﷺ added: "If somebody recites it during the day with firm faith in it, and dies on the same day before the evening, he will be from the people of Paradise; and if somebody recites it at night with firm faith in it, and dies before the morning, he will be from the people of Paradise." *"Fath al-Bari"* 11/97.

The Eighteenth Way

Offering Twelve voluntary Rak'ahs for Allah's Sake

On the authority of Umm Habibah, the Prophet ﷺ said: "Whoever prays twelve *Rak'ahs* during the day and night, Allah will built for him a house in Paradise: Four *Rak'ahs* before *Dhuhr* and two after it; two after *Maghreb Salaat*, two after *Isha'* and two before *Fajr*." At-Tirmidhi narrated this Hadith, see "*Sahih al-Ja'mi*'" 6362.

Spread Salaam, Feed the Poor, Show Kindness to Blood Relations and Offer Prayers at Night

The Prophet ﷺ said: "O people! Spread the _Salaam_ (greetings), feed (the poor and needy), behave kindly to your blood relations, offer prayers when others are asleep, and (thus) enter Paradise, in peace." Ibn Majah and other reported this Hadith, see: "_Sunan Ibn Majah_" 1097.

The Twentieth Way
Six Promises

On the authority of Ubadah Ibn as-Sa'mit ﷺ, the Prophet ﷺ said: "If you guarantee me six things on your part I shall guarantee you Paradise. Speak the truth when you talk, keep a promise when you make it, when you are trusted with something fulfil your trust, avoid sexual immorality, lower your eyes, and restrain your hands from injustice."

This Hadith is narrated by Ibn Khuzaimah, Ibn Hibban, al-Hakim and others; Sheikh Al-Bani classifies it as *Hadith Hasan* in his *"As-Silsila as-Sahihah"* 1470.

The Twenty-First Way

For Women

"Observing the five obligatory *Salaat* as Allah ﷻ has commanded, fasting during the month of *Ramadaan*, preserving her chastity and obeying her husband."

On the authority of Abu Hurairah ﷺ, Ibn Hibban reported in his "*Sahih*", that the Prophet ﷺ said: "When a woman observes the five daily prayers, fasts during *Ramadaan*, preserves her chastity and obeys her husband, she may enter by any of the gates of Paradise she wishes." "*Sahih al-Ja'mi*'" 660.

The Twenty-Second Way

Looking after Three Daughters or Sisters

On the authority of Anas ﷺ, Abu Ya'la' reported in his *"Musnad"*, the Prophet ﷺ said: "Whoever has three daughters or three sisters, cares for them and disciplines them, he and I shall be like these two in Paradise, putting the index finger and middle finger close together." *"Silsilat al-Ahadith as-Sahihah* 295".

Also, the Prophet ﷺ said: "If anyone treats well two slave girls, he and I shall be together like these two in Paradise, pointing two of his fingers." Sahih Muslim and Sunan at-Tirmidh, 4/281.

The Twenty-Third Way

Showing Patience when one's Children and Sincere Friends Die

The Prophet ﷺ said: "Whoever is bereaved of three offspring and anticipates Allah's rewards in the Hereafter, will enter Paradise." A woman said: "What about for only two." He ﷺ said: "And for two." An-Nisa'i' and Ibn Hibban reported it, see *"Sahih al-Ja'mi'"* 5969.

The Prophet ﷺ also said: "Any Muslim couple who are bereaved of three children who do not reach puberty yet, Allah will make them enter Paradise through His Mercy to them (the Muslim couple)." Imam Ahmed, an-Nisa'i' and Ibn Hibban narrated the Hadith, see: *"Sahih al-Jami'"* 5781.

Imam Ahmed reported in his *"Musnad"*, on the authority of Abu Hurairah ⲡ, that the Prophet ⲡ said: "Allah ⲡ says, 'If any of my believing slaves has a sincere friend in this life and I take his soul, and then he anticipates My Reward in the Hereafter, I shall reward him with Paradise." *"Sahih al-Ja'mi'"* 8139.

The Twenty-Fourth Way

Looking after an Orphan

On the authority of Sahl Ibn Sa'd, Imam al-Bukhari reported that the Prophet ﷺ said: "I and the person who looks after an orphan and provides for him, will be in Paradise like this, putting his index and middle fingers together." *"Fath al-Bari"* 1/436.

The Twenty-Fifth Way

Visit a Sick Person or a Brother in Islam

On the authority of Abu Hurairah ﷺ, the Prophet ﷺ said: "Whoever visits a sick person, or a brother in Islam for Allah's Sake, a caller will call him or her saying: 'May you and your visit be good, and you will get a honourable place in Paradise." This Hadith is reported by at-Tirmidhi, Ibn Majah and Sheikh al-Bani classifies it as *Hasan* in *"Sahih al-Ja'mi'"* 6387.

The Prophet ﷺ said: "The one who visits the sick is, in fact, like one who is in the fruit garden of Paradise, as long as he does not return." Imam Muslim reported it.

The Twenty-Sixth Way

Observing Two Qualities

On the authority of Abdullah Ibn Amru' ﷺ, the Prophet ﷺ said: "There are two qualities or characteristics which if any Muslim keeps, he will enter Paradise. While they are easy, those who act upon them are few. One should say: "Glory be to Allah" ten times, after every prayer; "Praise be to Allah" ten times, and "Allah is Most Great" ten times. That is a hundred and fifty on the tongue, but one thousand five hundred on the scale. When he goes to bed, he should say: "Allah is Most Great" thirty-four times, "Praise be to Allah" thirty-three times, and Glory be to Allah thirty-three times, for that is a hundred on the tongue, but a thousand on the scale. (He said:) I saw the Apostle of Allah ﷺ counting them on his hand. The people asked: 'Apostle of Allah! How is it that while they are easy, those who act upon them are few?' He ﷺ replied: 'Satan comes to one of you when he goes to bed and he makes him sleep, before he utters them, and he comes to him while he is engaged in prayer, and brings a need to his mind before he utters them.'" This Hadith is reported by Abu Dawud and at-Tirmidhi, who classified it as *"Hadith Hasan Sahih"*; an-Nisa'i' and Ibn Hibban in his *"Sahih"*, and *"Sahih at-Targheeb"* 603.

The Twenty-Seventh Way

Leniency in Buying and Selling

On the authority of Uthman Ibn Affan ﷺ, Imam al-Bukhari and Imam an-Nisa'i' reported that the Prophet ﷺ said: "Allah ﷻ admitted a man into Paradise because he was lenient in his buying, selling, paying back and in demanding his money back." *"Silsilat al-Ahadith as-Sahihah"* 1181.

The Twenty-Eighth Way

Showing Forgiveness to one's Debtor who is in Straitened Circumstances

On the authority of Abu Hurairah ﷺ, Imam Muslim reported in his "*Sahih*" that the Prophet ﷺ said: "There was a merchant who used to lend the people, and whenever his debtor was in straitened circumstances, he would say to his employees, 'Forgive him so that Allah may forgive us.' So, Allah forgave him."

The Twenty-Ninth Way

Four Good deeds, which help a Muslim enter Paradise, by Allah's Leave, if he has done them in one day

On the authority of Abu Hurairah ﷺ, Imam Muslim reported in his "*Sahih*" that the Prophet ﷺ said: "Who is fasting today?" Abu Bakr said: "Me". The Prophet ﷺ asked: "Who has followed a funeral procession today?" Abu Bakr said: "Me". The Prophet ﷺ asked again: "Who has fed a poor person today?" Abu Bakr said: "Me". The Prophet ﷺ then asked: "Who has visited a sick person today?" Abu Bakr replied: "Me". The

Prophet ﷺ then said: "Any person who has done these four things in one day will enter Paradise."

The Thirtieth Way

Showing Endurance and Seeking Allah's Reward for One's Loss of Sight

On the authority of Abu Hurairah ﷺ, the Prophet ﷺ said: "Allah ﷻ says: 'If I take away the sight of a Muslim, and he then shows endurance and seeks reward from Me, I shall be pleased with no lesser reward than Paradise for him.'" This Hadith is reported by at-Tirmidhi, see *"Sahih al-Ja'mi'"* 8140.

Women In Jahiliya & ISLAM

النساء في الجاهلية

DR. OMAR AHMED

DAJJAL THE FALSE MESSIAH

IMAM IBN KATHEER

ENJOINING GOOD FORBIDDING EVIL

SHEIKH AL-ISLAM IBN TAIMIYYAH

AL-FIRDOUS

THE RETURN OF

HIJAAB

PART I

DR. MUHAMMED IBN AHMED IBN ISMAIL

THE RETURN OF

HIJAAB

PART II

عودة الحجاب

DR. MUHAMMED IBN AHMED IBN ISMAIL

The
SEERAH
of
PROPHET MUHAMMAD
(S.A.W.)

Imam Ibn Kathīr

Abridged by:

Muhammad Ali Al-Halabi Al-Athari

PART II

TAFSĪR
IBN KATHĪR

PART 9

Sūrah Al-A'raaf, ayat 88 to 206
Sūrah Al-Anfal, ayat 1 to 40

ABRIDGED BY
Sheikh Muhammād Nasīb Ar-Rafā'ı

Al-Firdous Ltd., London

Winning the Heart of your Wife

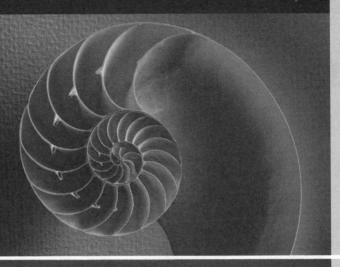

Ibraahim Ibn Saaleh al-Mahmud

الفردوس
AL-FIRDOUS